The Caribbean and Gulf of Mexico

The Caribbean and the Gulf of Mexico are everyone's idea of an ocean paradise. With their rocky, sun-drenched islands, palm-fringed beaches and beautiful coral reefs, it is no wonder that these seas have become an exotic playground for the holiday maker. But this is not all they have to offer. With the aid of over fifty pictures, this book describes the colourful inhabitants of the mainland and islands, the teeming plant and animal life to be found in the seas and mangrove swamps, and on the coral reefs, and the way we are exploiting the oil, fish, salt and other resources of the ocean. You can also learn about the volcanic structure of the islands, and how fierce hurricanes and tidal waves threaten their people. If the Cairibbn conjures up pictures of buccaneers and pieces of eight in your mind, you can read how pirates and smugglers once made their hide-outs in hidden caves and deserted coves along the shores. The book also contains a glossary, index and reading list.

SEAS AND OCEANS

The Caribbean
and Gulf of Mexico

Edited by Pat Hargreaves

WAYLAND

SILVER BURDETT

© Copyright 1980 Wayland Publishers Ltd

First published in 1980 by
Wayland Publishers Ltd
49 Lansdowne Place, Hove
East Sussex BN3 1HF, England

ISBN 0 85340 746 0

Published in the United States by
Silver Burdett Company
Morristown, New Jersey
1980 printing
ISBN 0 382 06469 0

Phototypeset by
Trident Graphics Limited, Reigate, Surrey
Printed in Italy by
G. Canale & C.S.p.A., Turin

Seas and Oceans

Three-quarters of the earth's surface is covered by sea. Each book in this series takes you on a cruise of a mighty ocean, telling you of its history, discovery and exploration, the people who live on its shores, and the animals and plants found in and around it.

The Atlantic
The Caribbean and Gulf of Mexico
The Mediterranean
The Antarctic
The Arctic
The Indian Ocean
The Red Sea and Persian Gulf
The Pacific

Contents

1 AN OCEAN PARADISE

The Caribbean Sea and the Gulf of Mexico are two large seas almost entirely encircled by land. Central America and part of South America form the Caribbean's borders to the south and west. A great curve of islands called the Antilles form its northern and eastern boundaries. Above this sea lies another sea, only about half as big. This is the Gulf of Mexico, which is bordered by the United States, Mexico and Cuba.

On your map you can see that Cuba lies across the entrance, joining the two seas. It is the first and largest of the great arc of islands that sweep east and south, ending with the island of Trinidad off the coast of Venezuela. East of Cuba you will find another large island of the Antillean chain called Hispaniola. This is divided into two separate countries: Haiti and the Dominican Republic. Further east you will see the Virgin Islands. They are much smaller than Cuba or Hispaniola, and you can see that the remaining islands of the Antilles are very small indeed. The names of some of these smaller islands – Dominica, Saba, the Grenadines – may remind you of pirates and explorers, for there are many exciting stories about the discovery and settling of the Antilles.

Cuba, Hispaniola, Puerto Rico and the Virgin Islands are called the Greater Antilles. Beyond the Virgin Islands lie the Lesser Antilles. The first large cluster of islands stretches south to Dominica. This part of the Lesser Antilles is sometimes called the Leeward Islands. The rest of the Lesser Antilles,

called the Windward Islands, stretch like stepping stones to the coast of South America. The names Leeward and Windward are used because sailing boats have a hard sail against the prevailing wind to get to Martinique, St Vincent, and other islands of the Windward group. The same boats have an easy sail with the wind, back towards the Leeward group.

Look at your map again. From Trinidad, the coasts of Colombia and Venezuela stretch 2,000 kilometres (1,500 miles) to the west. Then the Central American countries twist up toward Mexico. If you wish to sail from the Caribbean Sea into the Pacific Ocean you can go through the Panama Canal at the narrowest part of Central America. To complete your journey around the Caribbean you have only to travel up the Mexican coast to the Yucatan Peninsula. Now Cuba lies across the Yucatan Channel to the east.

Right Children gather around local fishing boats on a beach in Grenada.

The Antillean Islands are almost all very mountainous, and many of them are volcanic. But if you travel north of Cuba and Hispaniola you will find almost 700 small islands which are flat rather than mountainous. These are the islands of the Bahamas which lie on great shallow banks of sand and rock. Similarly, the mainland of the United States surrounding the Gulf of Mexico is quite flat, with broad, sandy beaches.

Throughout the islands, people depend on the sea a great deal. They travel from island to island in small boats loaded with local produce for the markets. These markets are often set up along quays where the boats can unload their wares. Goats, chickens, pigs, tomatoes, yams and coconuts are carried to market in this way. Here, fishermen also sell their bright tropical fish. Nearby, you might see a big sailing boat being built. This is one of the last areas in the world where sailing boats are still used for shipping cargoes and for fishing.

The weather is nearly always warm in the Caribbean. You need only light clothing, even at night. The clothes of the local people are bright and colourful, particularly the blouses and skirts of the women and girls. Everywhere you are reminded that you are in the tropics. In the market places you can see hats and other articles woven from palm leaves. There are ripe pineapples, sugar cane and bread fruit for sale. You would also see fruits you have probably never heard of, such as mangoes, guavas and sapodillas.

Above Bananas are an important commercial crop on many Caribbean islands.

Opposite Ruins of an ancient Maya shrine overlook the Gulf of Mexico at Tulum, on the Yucatan Peninsula.

9

Right Map of the Caribbean and the Gulf of Mexico.

GULF OF MEXICO

PACIFIC OCEAN

ATLANTIC OCEAN

Florida Straits

BAHAMAS

CUBA

Greater

Antilles

Channel

HISPANIOLA

DOMINICAN
REPUBLIC

HAITI

PUERTO RICO

Leeward Islands

CARIBBEAN

JAMAICA

Lesser Antilles

SEA

Windward Islands

Panama Canal

TRINIDAD

Moving continents and island arcs

In recent years the idea that continents move or drift around the surface of the earth has been accepted by scientists. Early map makers noticed that if the eastern edge of South America and the western edge of Africa were brought together, they would fit like pieces of a jigsaw puzzle. Further research showed that other land areas seemed to belong together. Fossils of similar land animals were found on both sides of the Atlantic Ocean. Since these land animals could not swim thousands of kilometres across the ocean, scientists decided that the continents must have been connected at some time, forming one or more huge supercontinents. They thought that some continents, including South America and Africa, had drifted apart leaving a great ocean between them.

Below The Earth's crust is made up of six to eight main plates. Where these plates collide or move apart, they unleash volcanoes and earthquakes. The red triangles represent the present areas of volcanic activity.

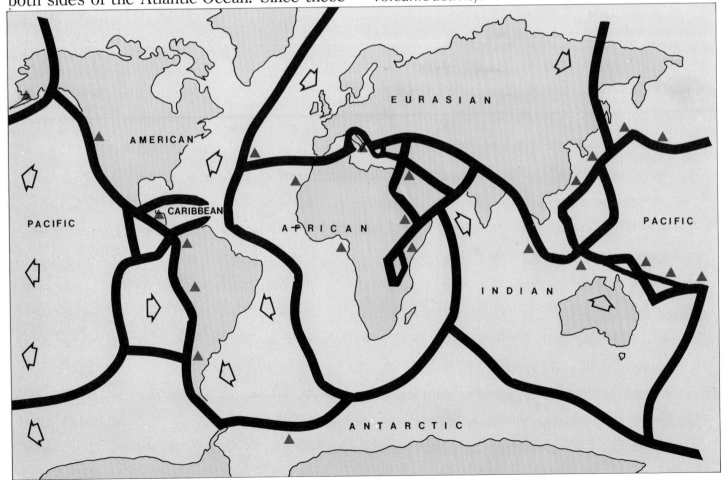

At first it was thought that the continents simply moved freely across the Earth's surface. Then scientific experiments showed that a huge underwater mountain chain (the Mid-Atlantic Ridge) zig-zagged along the floor of the Atlantic Ocean. There were also undersea trenches and volcanoes. Could these geological features have something to do with the movement of the continents? A scientific research ship called the *Glomar Challenger* was sent to the South Atlantic to investigate. Drillers lowered pipes into the sea and took samples of rocks and sediments from the ocean floor. Careful studies of these samples revealed that the ocean floor was gradually spreading away from the Mid-Atlantic Ridge. The rock samples got older the farther away from the Ridge they were found. Rocks a few kilometres away were millions of years old.

In fact, hot molten rock (magma) is constantly rising from the interior of the Earth through the sea floor at the Ridge. It cools and becomes attached to the rest of the rock, forming the sea floor. This itself moves away as more lava is added. It is now known that the rock forming the sea floor in fact covers the whole of the Earth, and that it is split into large, rigid sections called plates. The continents lie on top of the plates and if the plates move so do the continents.

Although new material from the Earth's interior is being constantly added to the floor of the ocean, the plates are not increasing in size. The reason for this is that in areas where two

Above Submersibles like this one are used for all kinds of underwater research. They need powerful lights to see in the great depths of the ocean where sunlight never penetrates.

plates meet, they may move over or under one another. The edge of one plate is destroyed as it moves down and under another one. This occurs at a 'trench'. As the plates move along they scrape against each other causing earthquakes. Rubbing of the plates together also produces heat and melts the surrounding rock. The molten rock may move upwards under pressure and form a volcano. Sometimes the volcano lies under the sea but others can also rise above the surface. Chains of volcanic islands can be made in this way. They are called island arcs because they are often arranged in curves.

Left Volcanic rock litters the slopes of Monserrat's volcano.

There is still much to find out about the origins of the Gulf of Mexico and the Caribbean. In parts of the Gulf of Mexico, salt deposits have been found in the sea floor. Such deposits might have occurred from the evaporation of water from a shallow, salty sea. So it is possible that millions of years ago the Gulf was a separate, land-locked sea, cut off from the Caribbean and the Atlantic Ocean. If so, then Florida and the Yucatan Peninsula may once have been joined, forming a boundary.

The origin of the Caribbean Sea is much more complicated. It lies over the Caribbean Plate. (Remember, plates are large blocks of rock forming the sea floor and lying under the continents.) The Caribbean Plate is surrounded by trenches, earthquake zones and volcanoes. Scientists believe that those islands in the Caribbean called the Lesser Antilles are island arcs formed by volcanic activity. However, there is still much to be learned about the geology of the area.

14

Above If the Caribbean and Gulf of Mexico were drained of their water you would be able to see these mountain ranges, ridges and deep basins which make up the sea floor.

15

Sediments and rocks

Above The coastal waters of the Caribbean and the Gulf of Mexico abound with coral reefs.

Sediments which have piled up in the Gulf of Mexico and the Caribbean come from a variety of sources. The oldest and deepest sediments in the Gulf are salts. In the shallow lagoons and seas, the sun can evaporate large quantities of water leaving deposits of salt behind. After a time, returning sea-water covers up the salt. If a thick sediment layer forms over the salt it may squeeze the salt up towards the surface. These mounds of salt are called salt domes. Oil is often trapped beside these domes, so oil companies are interested in them.

Fine particles of clay also settle on the bottom. In the deep basins of the ocean these sediments form very thick layers. In parts of the Caribbean Sea there are up to 2,000 metres (6,500 ft) of sediment. Reefs form in shallow water near land (see Chapter 7). Some islands themselves were formed as a result of many years of reef build-up.

Sometimes, where rivers flow into the sea, they carry sediments eroded from the land to the ocean. In the northern part of the Gulf of Mexico, the Mississippi River has deposited huge amounts of mud and sand into the sea around its mouth. Currents flowing along the coast in this area have piled some of this sediment into a string of islands.

The kinds of sediments found in deep seas include the skeletons of tiny marine plants and animals called plankton. One kind of tiny animal, called globigerina, lives at the sea surface, but has a skeleton that sinks. The skeletons of globigerina have produced much of the sea-floor sediment at depths of between 3,000 and 4,000 metres (10,000 and 13,000 ft). Below these depths, globigerina skeletons dissolve.

Mixed with all these sediments are other solid materials: sharks' teeth, the bones and skulls of whales, even tiny pieces of iron meteorites have been found. Oceanographers have also found milk bottles and other rubbish scattered about in the ocean depths.

Below The muddy waters of the Mississippi River at New Orleans. The Mississippi deposits a huge amount of mud and sand into the Gulf of Mexico.

3 THE EARLY SETTLERS

Explorers and traders

The islands of the Caribbean were discovered by Christopher Columbus in 1492. On 12th October, he sighted the island of San Salvador, but thought that he had found one of the many islands off the coast of Japan. Sailing on through the Bahamas and past Cuba, he ran aground off Hispaniola on Christmas Day. The brown-skinned natives he found there he called 'Indians'.

Columbus made his discoveries in the name of the King of Spain, and for most of the sixteenth century Spanish settlers and explorers dominated the Caribbean. To begin with, the lure of gold from Hispaniola and Cuba attracted large numbers of settlers. When this gold ran out, the Caribbean islands were chiefly used as bases from which expeditions sailed to explore Central America and Mexico. Their importance was increased when the Spanish began shipping large quantities of Mexican and Peruvian silver back to Europe. The Spanish had to organize their ships into carefully guarded convoys, as famous adventurers like Sir Francis Drake were always ready to pounce on an undefended treasure ship.

At last Spain's naval strength began to fade, and other nations began to explore and settle in the Caribbean and the Gulf. English, Dutch and French settlers fought for possession of the valuable islands in the Leeward and Windward chains. These islands were very important to European merchants because they were the focal point of what was known as the 'triangular trade'. Trading ships sailed from Europe to pick up a human cargo of slaves from bases on the West African coast. These slaves were exchanged in the Caribbean for sugar and rum, which were then brought back to markets in European countries.

Below Early Spanish settlers land on a Caribbean island.

Above French explorers claim the island of Martinique for the King of France in 1625.

Right Diver with a 'piece of eight' from the wreck of a Spanish galleon.

So valuable was this trade, that every European war in the eighteenth century was accompanied by heavy fighting in the Caribbean; and every peace treaty included the exchange of Caribbean islands. Before the Battle of Trafalgar in 1805, Admiral Nelson was forced to chase the French fleet all the way to the Caribbean and back in order to protect British colonies there.

Above Sailors brand slaves, before shipping them to work on sugar plantations in the Caribbean.

Sugar plantations and slaves

The original natives of the Caribbean islands were the gentle Arawak Indians. These peaceful Arawaks were soon taken over by fiercer Indians from South America. One such warlike tribe was the 'Carib' Indians – an Arawak word which means 'cannibal'.

Early Caribbean settlers tried to use the native Indians for field labour, but the Arawaks were not hardy enough and died out, and the Caribs would not submit to such lowly work. Sugar was now very popular in Europe. The Dutch brought their sugar-making secrets to the islands in the 1640s, and within ten years sugar cane was the major Caribbean crop. Large plantations sprang up, and with them came a great demand for slave labour.

England, France, Holland and Portugal set up slave bases on the coast of West Africa. Negroes were rounded up on the beaches and were chained in the holds of slave ships for the voyage back to the New World. The slaves were often forced to work on the sugar plantations under brutal conditions. Some slaves, such as those on the island of Haiti, eventually gained their freedom by revolting against their masters. But most were forced to wait until European governments abolished the slave system in their colonies. For the British

Below You can see from these plans how tightly slave ships were packed for the voyage across the Atlantic. Some slaves lay in lines, chained head to foot, while others had to crouch on narrow shelves which ran around the hull. Many died on the journey.

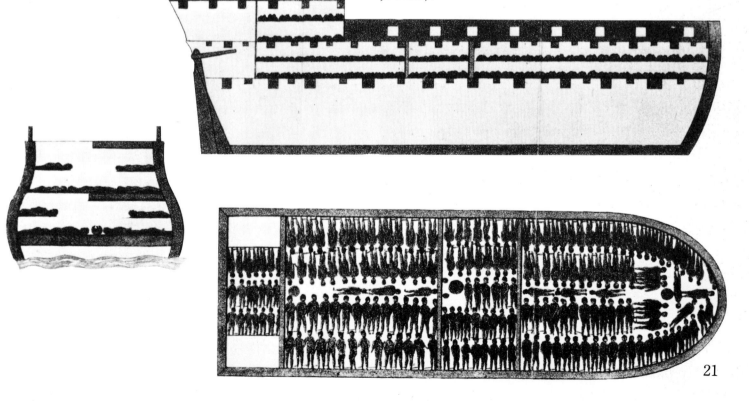

colonies this was finally achieved in 1838, but those under Spanish masters, in Cuba and Puerto Rico, were not set free until 1898.

Plantation owners also made use of 'indentured servants' from various countries. These were usually European labourers who agreed to work for seven years without pay in return for their ocean passage to the colonies. During the English Civil War (1642–9), almost 80,000 people came to the Caribbean from England, many as indentured servants. They were often treated worse than the slaves themselves.

During the earliest days of colonization, a great many smugglers and pirates were happy to settle in the Gulf and around the Caribbean. The islands contain small, well-hidden coves which were perfect hiding-places for landing goods, or to use as bases from which to raid other ships.

The end of slavery meant that the plantation owners had to recruit workers for their fields. Almost half a million Chinese and East Indians came to the West Indies in the 1900s. Some people came from Europe too, and new settlers came from Sweden and Denmark.

Today, most of the islands have their own governments. Some of them still maintain links with their old colonial rulers, but the larger ones like Jamaica, Barbados and Trinidad are completely independent.

Above Even today much of the sugar cane is harvested by hand. Here a labourer uses the traditional long 'machete' knife.

Right Old sugar mill on the island of Montserrat.

4 THE MOVING WATERS

The weather and the water

In the Caribbean Sea, the warm trade winds blow steadily all the year round from the east. When the moist, warm trade wind blows up a cool mountainside the tiny drops of water in the air join together to form rain drops and there is a torrential downpour.

Further north, in the Gulf of Mexico, the wind is more changeable. In the summer there is often no breeze at all. In the winter, cold weather moves down from Canada and Alaska, bringing strong north winds and chilly days.

In the summer and early autumn, great storms arise in the Caribbean Sea and in the Atlantic to the east. These storms, called hurricanes, may be more than 160 kilometres (100 miles) across and can cause great damage. Warm, moist air blows from all directions towards the hurricane. When the air reaches the storm, it blows around the centre or 'eye'

Below Palm trees in the streets of Corpus Christi, Texas, are blown down by winds from a hurricane sweeping in across the Gulf of Mexico.

Above This picture, taken from one of the Apollo spacecraft, shows the distinctive 'catherine wheel' shape of a hurricane moving across the Gulf of Mexico. Can you find the 'eye' of the storm?

of the storm. The warm wind rises and cools, but is replaced by more air blowing in across the sea surface which continues to feed the storm. In a week or two a hurricane may move more than 1,600 kilometres (1,000 miles).

Warm, moist air is necessary for hurricanes, and eventually they are broken up and halted by mountains or by cool air found over land.

The water of the Caribbean Sea and Gulf of Mexico is quite warm. The water temperature averages 25°C throughout the year. Beneath the surface, below a depth of about 60 metres (200 ft), there is a much cooler layer. The warm surface water is not as heavy as this cool water and so it floats on top of it although if it is very salty it will tend to sink.

The deep water in the Caribbean is cold water that has come from the Atlantic Ocean from depths of about 1,800 metres (6,000 ft) through a deep channel called the Anegada Passage.

The amount of salt we find dissolved in sea-water varies slightly from place to place. The saltiness (salinity) is greatest in shallow areas where the sun evaporates the water and leaves salt behind.

25

Currents

Near the Equator, warm, tropical trade winds move the ocean water in two strong currents. These are called the North and South Equatorial Currents. They are like two rivers flowing through the Atlantic Ocean. The North Equatorial Current carries warm tropical water between the islands of the Lesser Antilles into the Caribbean Sea. Brazil splits the South Equatorial Current and part of that also passes into the Caribbean. If you lived on a Caribbean island you would be thankful for the trade winds and the Equatorial Currents. They are responsible for the tropical climate there.

The Caribbean surface water moves towards Central America, and some of this Caribbean Current, as it is called, pours between Cuba and Mexico. This passage is called the Yucatan Channel, and the water passing through the Channel runs into the Gulf of Mexico. In the Gulf, the water makes a big loop up towards the Mississippi River delta and then sweeps between Florida and Cuba. Here, in the Straits of Florida, it becomes one of the strongest ocean currents of all. Sometimes this Florida Current flows almost as fast as you can run.

Not all of the water from the Equatorial Currents goes into the Caribbean Sea. Some of it passes east of the Caribbean islands and up past the islands of the Bahamas. This part, called the Antilles Current, joins the Florida Current north of the Bahamas. The combination of these two currents produces the Gulf Stream. While the Florida Current is one of the fastest ocean currents, the Gulf Stream is one of the biggest. Along the coast of the United States it carries 75 times as much water as all the rivers on Earth. The Gulf Stream carries warm water all the way to the British Isles and the coast of Norway.

Below The trade winds and the equatorial currents are responsible for the warm climate in much of the Caribbean. These small boys are making the most of it.

Right Diagram showing the major currents in the Caribbean and the Gulf of Mexico.

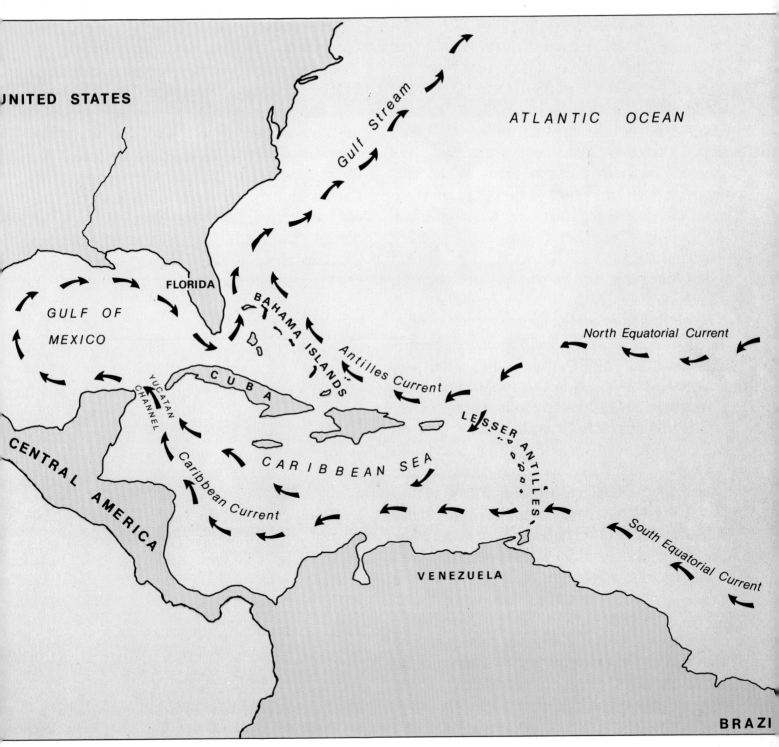

UNITED STATES

ATLANTIC OCEAN

Gulf Stream

FLORIDA

GULF OF MEXICO

BAHAMA ISLANDS

North Equatorial Current

Antilles Current

YUCATAN CHANNEL

CUBA

LESSER ANTILLES

CENTRAL AMERICA

CARIBBEAN SEA

Caribbean Current

VENEZUELA

South Equatorial Current

BRAZIL

27

Waves, tides and 'tsunami' waves

If the wind blows steadily from one direction it can cause surface currents. You have seen that the North and South Equatorial Currents are created by the trade winds. These same trade winds also make waves which move into the Caribbean from the Atlantic. When the waves reach shallow water, near land, they are slowed down by the sea floor. When this happens, the back side of the wave runs up over the front and forms a foaming white breaker. It is very exciting to see these big waves crashing against the coral reefs and rocky shores on the eastern sides of Caribbean islands on a windy day.

Sometimes waves wear away caves under the cliffs of islands, so that the water crashes into the cave and squirts up on to the land through 'blow-holes' in the roof of the cave. These blow-holes are great tourist attractions.

The pull of gravity from the Sun and Moon causes tides in the sea. Tides are changes in sea level. Tides are not very great in the Caribbean or Gulf of Mexico. Many of the Antillean Islands have a tide range of only about 30 centimetres (1 ft) or less, from high to low tide. In the islands of the Bahamas and the Gulf of Mexico the range can be as much as one metre (about 3 ft), and along the coast of South America there are places where three metre (9 ft) tides are found. Usually there are two high and two low tides every 24 hours. In the Gulf of Mexico there are places where at times there is only one high tide and one low tide a day.

Tidal waves have nothing to do with everyday tides. The scientific name for them is 'tsunami' waves, and they are caused by volcanic eruptions or earthquakes. In the open sea, these waves are quite low, and you might not notice them from a ship. But when they funnel into shallow shores they can tower up to 65 metres (210 ft) high. The people of the Caribbean have good reason to fear tsunamis, as they can cause enormous damage and destruction. In 1692 a great earthquake and tsunami plunged the Jamaican capital (then Port Royal) into the sea.

Right Atlantic rollers sweep in to the shore on the east coast of Barbados.

Above Shrimp boats in harbour at Key West, Florida. They form part of America's huge shrimp-fishing fleet that operates in the Gulf of Mexico.

Fish and fishing

Among the many islands of the Caribbean Sea, only Cuba and Puerto Rico have modern fishing fleets of any size. Cuba has a number of very big trawlers which work far out to sea and freeze their fish on board. They fish in the Gulf of Mexico, catching croaker and many other types of fish which are never seen in Europe. Cuba's annual catch is about 180,000 tonnes. Many of Puerto Rico's big fishing boats work for American fish-packing companies. They travel thousands of kilometres in search of tuna fish, which they freeze on board. Nearer home, other boats catch sardines. The country's annual catch of all fish is about 80,000 tonnes.

Fishermen in the other Caribbean islands mostly use small boats and canoes with outboard motors. They fish with lines, nets and traps for all kinds of tropical fish and shellfish. Their catch is usually sold to fishermen's co-operatives and to local merchants, and it is eaten by the local people.

The Gulf of Mexico, to the north, is so rich in fish and shellfish that it is sometimes called the Fertile Fish Crescent. The biggest catch of all is a fish rather like a herring, called menhaden. Each year, 450,000 tonnes of this and other 'industrial' fish are made into 'fish-meal' which

Right On the islands, fish is bought and sold right on the sea shore. This fisherman's wife weighs some red snappers for a local hotel.

is fed to farm animals, or canned as pet food. The oil extracted from menhaden is also valuable and is used to make margarine and lipsticks. Menhaden fishing is so important that spotter planes are used to search for the oily patches of water which lie on the surface above the shoals of fish.

The mainland countries which border the Gulf and Caribbean are well suited for fish farming. Fish and shellfish grow faster in hot climates; land is cheap and there are plenty of people willing to work. This means that trout, catfish and prawns can be grown in large quantities at a low cost.

Right Local fishermen land their catch on a beach in Grenada.

Shellfish and turtles

The Caribbean Sea and Mexican Gulf together produce more than 166,000 tonnes of shellfish each year. Most of this – 150,000 tonnes – is shrimp from the Gulf, which is the world's biggest shrimp fishery. Most of this is caught by hundreds of shrimp trawlers from Texas and Mexico. Cuba, Nicaragua, Panama and other nations take a smaller share. These trawlers are about 20 metres (66 ft) long and they tow two or three nets.

The waters of the Gulf are rich with food and minerals carried down to the sea by the Mississippi River, and the shallow, sandy sea-bed is ideal for shellfish. Stone crabs, blue crabs and spiny lobsters are caught in traps; oysters, clams and scallops are dredged from the sea-bed, and squid and cuttlefish are caught in trawls.

The warm sea and reefs around Cuba, Haiti, Puerto Rico and many smaller islands provide ideal homes for prawns and spiny lobsters – sometimes called crawfish or langouste. In the mainland countries of Nicaragua, Colombia and Venezuela, prawns ten centimetres (4 in.) long – or as big as your hand – are being grown in shallow ponds on special 'farms'. In a warm climate, where cheap land and labour are available, it is more economical to farm prawns

Left Shrimps are big business in the Gulf of Mexico. At Key West, Florida, they are fed on to a conveyor belt before being sorted and packed for the American market.

Above A Green turtle hatchling begins its perilous journey to the sea. Many young turtles are picked off by seabirds before they reach the water.

in this way than to send out boats to catch them.

The green turtle is also being farmed in the Caribbean. This is one of five kinds of sea turtle found in this area, and it – and its eggs – provide food for the local people. The flesh is made into turtle soup. The shells are also useful for making beautiful 'tortoise-shell' jewellery, and the skins are made into leather goods. Because they are so valuable, too many turtles are caught, and this means they are becoming scarce. The eggs, which the female lays in the sand by the sea shore, are often stolen by man or eaten by animals and birds. Sea birds also swoop down and pick off the tiny turtles as they hatch out and make for the sea. Green turtles are now kept in special hatcheries, where their eggs can hatch in safety.

One of Shell's oil rigs in the Gulf of Mexico.

Oil and power from the sea

Oil can be found in shallow water along parts of coastal South America and in the Gulf of Mexico. Drilling an oil well in the sea is a difficult operation, but it can be done. Great platforms, with long legs that perch on the sea floor, are used to support the drilling equipment. Divers are needed to install the equipment. Their work is very dangerous and they sometimes get hurt or even killed while working under-water. After the well is drilled, people live on the platforms and supervise the pumping of the oil. Such oil platforms can be seen in Lake Maracaibo (in Venezuela) and around the Gulf of Mexico from the Yucatan Peninsula to Texas.

Some people are afraid that drilling will harm the plants and animals which live in and around the sea. If oil is spilled, or if it leaks out of the wells, it floats and often washes ashore, polluting the beaches. Sea birds which get oil on their feathers often die, and so do some animals which live on the sea shore and are covered in oil. Detergents are used to clean up the spilled oil, for if it is left alone it takes many months to break up and disappear.

The Caribbean is one of the oceans of the world considered suitable for installing OTECs (Ocean Thermal Electric Conversion devices). These are power-plants which generate electricity by exploiting the temperature difference between the very warm surface water and the cold layers below. The energy created could be piped to land by underwater cables running along the ocean floor. The first modern OTEC is now operating off Hawaii in the Pacific. A full-size version could provide enough power for a city of 20,000 people. OTECs may soon be a very important source of electricity. The U.S. Department of Energy is supporting research connected with them.

Below Oil spillage from tankers can be fatal to seabirds.

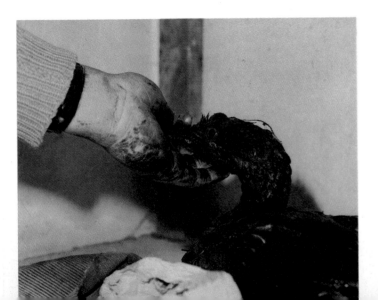

Below One of the many designs for OTEC. It generates electricity by exploiting the temperature differences in the sea.

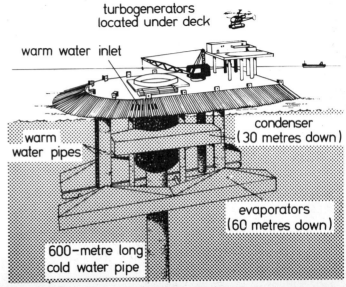

Sand, shells, pearls, coral and salt

Different Caribbean islands and countries have found other resources in the sea apart from fish and oil. For example, the biggest natural resource of the Bahamas is sand! Bahamian sand can be used for manufacturing bricks, cement, lime and other building materials. Where the sand is pumped up from the sea floor it has actually been piled up to make an island called Ocean Cay. Here it can be easily loaded on to trucks and carried to barges for the trip across the Straits of Florida to the mainland.

Throughout the Caribbean Islands, beautiful seashells are collected and sold to tourists. There are hundreds of different kinds, with delicate colours and strange shapes. Pearl oysters live in shallow water in most parts of the Caribbean, and along the Venezuelan coast. These are harvested for their pearls, which are sometimes quite large. Since the

Below Solar salt pan on Bonaire Island.

Above Some of the beautiful shells found around the coast of Florida.

oyster lives in very shallow water, it can be collected easily by wading or diving.

Near the coast of Mexico, divers collect a kind of coral with a shiny, jet-black skeleton, which can be made into jewellery. Elsewhere, other types of corals are collected and sold as souvenirs. But, as coral grows rather slowly, its collection must be controlled so that the reefs are not destroyed (see Chapter 7).

In the eastern Bahamas, where very little rain falls, there are islands where salt is produced with the help of the sun. Sea-water is allowed to run into shallow ponds and then the entrance to the sea is shut off. The hot sun evaporates the water, and the salt which is left is shovelled into sacks. It is then sold to companies which package it into boxes so that you can sprinkle it over your food.

Irrigation and desalination

Above The Blue Mountains of Jamaica receive plenty of rainfall, as the dense, green vegetation illustrates.

Some islands in the Caribbean get very little rain. Often these are low islands, and so the wind blows right over them without dropping any rain. Larger, more mountainous islands make the moist air rise. This air then cools and rain forms. But even these islands may get little water beyond the coastal mountains, because by the time the air has crossed them, it has already been robbed of its rain. On the windward sides of such islands there are rain forests. But on the other sides there may be deserts.

Fresh water can be run through pipes or ditches from wet areas to the dry parts. Then successful farming can be carried out on otherwise barren land. This process is called irrigation. The Samana peninsula of the Dominican Republic has become an important producer of rice as a result of careful irrigation. Since rice grows in shallow water, low walls have been built around the fields. Water is then run into the fields and is held in by the walls.

Although there are certainly big differences in rainfall on Caribbean islands, which cause drought in some areas, man has also been responsible for water shortages. When the first settlers came, they often cut down the forests and planted sugar cane. The destruction of the forests weakened the soil, which was gradually washed away. Soon many of the islands became very rocky. With little or no soil to hold water in the ground, such islands became desert-like. In some places fresh water may have to be brought from elsewhere

in ships. Today the problem is often solved by using sea-water. Although it is difficult to remove the salt from sea-water to make it fresh, it can be done. This process is called desalination. Desalination plants supply drinking water at the United States naval base at Guantanamo, on the island of Cuba, in the Virgin Islands, on the island of Aruba, and at Key West, Florida.

Above Sugar cane cutters on Barbados. There are sugar plantations on most islands in the Caribbean.

41

Above Golden clumps of sargassum weed float everywhere in the Caribbean. Many tiny sea creatures can be found clinging to the protective weed.

Surface plants and animals

In the oceans, only the thin layer of surface water receives enough sunlight for plants to grow. Besides sunlight, plants need minerals such as nitrogen and phosphorus. In the clear water of the Caribbean, sunlight penetrates to depths of 250 metres (820 ft) or more, but there is not much nitrogen or phosphorus. Compared with other oceans, the Caribbean Sea is not particularly rich in marine life. The water is not green with tiny plants, but is very clear.

However, enough tiny plants and animals drift about to provide food for many kinds of larger animals. The drifting plants and animals are called plankton, and some of them are not as small as you might think. Large golden clumps of seaweed called sargassum float everywhere on blue Caribbean water. Sargassum can be called plankton because it drifts. It provides shelter for dozens of tiny shrimps, crabs and baby fish. Larger fish often swim along with drifting sargassum. They feed on the little creatures hiding amongst the seaweed.

The Portuguese man-of-war is also a large member of the plankton family. It is a kind of great jellyfish with a bright blue float filled with gas. It uses this to drift along with the winds and currents. You would not want to touch it, for beneath the float trail stinging tentacles three to ten metres (10 to 33 ft) long. Other jellyfish drift about beneath the surface. They are accompanied by many kinds of small

Above Large shoal of snappers in the Caribbean.

crustacean animals called copepods, by baby fish, and by planktonic animals and plants too small to see without a microscope.

Near the islands and mainland there are big fish such as sailfish, marlin, tuna, mackerel and sharks. Beautiful fish called dolphins (not the bottle-nosed dolphins you see in 'Dol- phinariums', which are not fish but mammals like whales) leap from the water to chase flying fish. Of course flying fish cannot really fly. They jump into the air to escape larger fish and glide above the sea on wide, wing-like fins. Schools of whales and dolphins occasionally enter the Caribbean from the Atlantic.

Life in the middle and great depths

Beneath the sun-lit surface waters, from 1,000 to 4,000 metres (3,280 to 13,000 ft) down, is a region which receives no light from the sun. The only light down here comes from small fish, shrimp and squid, which have tiny lamps, called light organs, on their bodies. They are like underwater fireflies. There are a number of reasons why these creatures might need light organs.

Many kinds of fish, shrimp, and squid, seem to have their own special pattern of lights on their bodies. Perhaps they can recognize these patterns and stay together in groups with others of their own kind. Some light organs seem to produce a very bright flash of light. Such a bright flash might blind an enemy and allow time for escape.

The colours of mid-water animals are interesting. Most of the shrimps are bright scarlet. Mid-water fish are often black or silvery. Some, with their patterns of green, yellow and white light organs, are quite beautiful. Some, like the viper fish, have enormous fang-like teeth. Almost all can eat very large meals, and some can even eat a fish larger than themselves. This is very important to a fish which may only find a meal once a week or so.

Many kinds of squid live in the Caribbean and the Gulf. The best known is the giant squid, which may have a body two metres (6 ft) long and tentacles over 12 metres (40 ft) long. Giant squid seem to live in rather shallow water. Many small squid live in mid-water regions below 1,000 metres (3,280 ft). Some are covered with light organs which look like tiny jewels. The vampire squid has only four light organs and is about 30 centimetres (1 ft) long. It is black and has tentacles joined together by a web.

Below Pop-eyed squid in defensive attitude. It is covered in 'jewels' – tiny patches of light produced by chemicals in its body.

Right A type of angler fish in sargassum weed.

You would find fewer animals with light organs in the very deepest waters of the Caribbean Sea and Gulf of Mexico. Here the fish and shrimp are often without colour and may have no eyes. On the sea floor there are many kinds of animals which do not live in mid-water. You would see dozens of starfish and brittlestars. Perhaps a large blind lobster would be walking slowly past. Small shrimp lie quietly in the mud. The shrimp here often have rather thick, hard shells. Many of the animals which live on the bottom eat mud. The mud alone is not a food, but it is full of microscopic creatures called bacteria. These bacteria do not need sunlight to help them grow, so they can live in the dark, deep water.

Many kinds of shark live down near the sea floor. One is the cat shark. It has pale green eyes and a beautiful pattern of tan markings. You would not have to worry about this shark for it is only 30 centimetres (1 ft) long.

The sea floor is made up of particles called sediment. Many tiny marine animals and plants produce skeletons that sink to the sea floor and help make this sediment. You can read more about sediments in Chapter 2.

Left Spiny lobster in shallow water off the Bahamas. Every autumn these animals take part in an amazing migration. The lobsters form long lines in single file, each animal grasping the tail of the lobster in front. In this fashion, they make their way to the relative safety of deep water to spawn.

Above Blood starfish – so called because of its dark red colour – crawls over shells and sponges. It moves by means of tiny tube-like 'feet' beneath its arms.

Coral reefs are built by simple animals, much like jellyfish. They do not drift like jellyfish, but live attached to the bottom. Their mouths and tentacles point upward. Though most coral animals cannot sting you, their tentacles have stinging structures which sting and help to capture small planktonic animals. This plankton is their food. But strangely, some coral animals cannot seem to get enough food from plankton alone. To help them survive, the kinds of coral animals that live on reefs have millions of tiny (microscopic) plant cells living in their bodies. Each of these cells is a complete, very simple, green plant. Of course they have no flowers, roots or branches, but they behave in much the same way as more complicated plants. Each of these cells can use the sun's energy to manufacture its food of simple sugars and starches. It also uses some of the waste material of the coral animal for its fertilizer. These cells help the coral animal by 'leaking' some of their own food back to the animal. When a plant and animal work together in such a fashion, it is called *symbiosis* (which is a word that means 'life together').

A single coral animal, called a polyp, can split itself and make two polyps. Now imagine how

Above Solitary cup coral with tentacles extended for capturing food.

many polyps there might be if those two split to make four, and the four split to make eight, and so on. Soon there would be thousands of polyps. This is how the coral animals increase. Most of these animals live together in huge colonies. From time to time the coral polyp releases a tiny larva which crawls or drifts away to grow into a new polyp. In this way it is possible for new colonies to grow far away from the parent colony.

Left Assorted soft and hard corals grow side by side on a shallow reef.

49

Sea-water has a great deal of limestone dissolved in it. As coral polyps grow they are able to use the lime to build a skeleton of limestone. Only the surface of the skeleton is covered by living polyps. Because the coral animals live a very long time, the skeleton may become very thick. Some corals build large boulders of skeleton, others make branching 'trees'. A few make small round 'pebbles', and those that live as single polyps just make a stone cup. There are almost a hundred different kinds of 'stony' coral in the Caribbean, but not all corals make a skeleton of stone. The lovely purple, red, or blue sea 'fans' and sea 'feathers' (called gorgonids) are soft and flexible. In the Caribbean, both stony and soft corals, build coral reefs.

Where the water is shallow and clear, many kinds of coral can grow together. Boulders of living coral may cover only a small part of the bottom, but the huge rock boulders made by earlier colonies lie about everywhere. There are always many tunnels and caves between and under such mounds of coral boulders. The deepest parts of these caves gradually fill with sand and mud. In time, the mud becomes stone and helps cement the reef together. Along the edges of deep water, facing the waves, the reefs may be over 160 kilometres (100 miles) long. There are often pleasant, shallow lagoons lying behind these long, wide reefs. In such lagoons you may also find small, round patches of coral.

Many kinds of plants and animals live together on the reefs. Red and yellow sponges, soft and stony corals and flower-like anemones are everywhere. There are many hiding places for the brightly coloured fish and lobsters. Sharks and barracudas that visit the reef by day have a hard time catching their food. At night some of these bright reef animals swim or crawl away to feed in nearby seaweed patches. At first light of dawn they hurry back to the safety of the reef.

Not all reef animals feed at night. During the day, parrot fish scrape away rock with their hard, shiny 'beaks'. They actually swallow the rock, but their food is the thin coating of plant life on the rock's surface. Surgeon fish eat the bigger seaweeds that grow everywhere. Little black-and-gold striped sergeant-major fish swim above the reef and snap at the planktonic animals that drift about. A Spanish hogfish picks small parasites off other fish. Nearby, a tiny shrimp sways back and forth on the tentacles of a sea anemone. It too is a parasite picker. When a fish swims near, the shrimp hops on its back and scurries about looking for parasites. The fish always seem to realize that the shrimp and the hogfish are helping them. They rest quietly while the little parasite pickers do their work.

It would be exciting for you to visit a coral reef some day if you possibly can. They are so beautiful and there is so much to see in the clear, warm water.

Right Great barracuda can often be seen hovering around coral reefs in search of prey. They have long, streamlined bodies which enable them to swim very fast. They are ferocious when attacking other fish.

Below Spanish hogfish sees off a potential rival.

8 THE SEA SHORE

Rocky shores and sandy beaches

Along the Caribbean coasts, there are rocky cliffs or broad ledges of rock. At the water's edge the rough surface of the rock is encrusted with animals and thin films of algae. At low tide many of the animals seek shelter from the sun in cracks and crevices in the rocks. Tide pools offer shelter for hermit crabs and small fish. High on the shore, where the high tides just reach, nerite snails and beaded periwinkles clamp themselves firmly to the rock.

Nearer the sea, barnacles shut their shells tightly while they wait for the water to return. One kind of sea urchin scrapes shallow holes in the rocks with its spines and hard jaws. Here it is protected from the sun and the fury of the waves. When the tide comes in all the rocky shore animals roam about in search of food while they can. In a few hours the tide will have fallen again.

Along the seaward edge of the rocky shore, chunks of rock have been carved and tumbled by the wave's force. Pebble crabs, hermit crabs and colourful snails hide amongst the rocks. Delicate lavender tube sponges and brown chicken-liver sponges encrust the rocks where the waves are not too strong. Great

Right Ghost crabs make a meal of a dead fish washed ashore by the tide. These crabs live in burrows on the shore and can move surprisingly fast in pursuit of their prey.

Left Although it may look just like a beautiful plant, this sea anemone has stinging tentacles to capture passing fish. The fish are then eaten.

Above Young black-headed gull picks around for food in the incoming tide.

clumps of seaweed grow here at the low tide mark. Golden sargassum and bright green feathery or bead-like caulerpa form a bright carpet. Frilly green and purple clusters of tiny colourful colonial anemones also live along the outer edges of the rock. The animals and plants near the low tide mark need not worry about the sun, for they are almost always covered by water.

Narrow belts of sandy beaches border many Caribbean shores while wider beaches are found around the Gulf of Mexico. The sands are often made of bits and pieces of coral and shells. If you sift about you may find beautiful shells, pieces of coral or even a shark's tooth.

Seaweed and seagrass debris, left by the high tide, lines the shore. It is the home of thousands of leaping, shrimp-like 'sand hop-pers', which share the decaying grass with burrowing worms and a few small snails. Large ghost crabs live in burrows near the line of decaying seaweed. At dawn and dusk they wander about, looking for something to eat.

At the water's edge mole crabs burrow just beneath the sand surface. Tiny coqunia clams with shiny pink, yellow and purple shells, filter plankton from the water washing about them. A little further down, below the low tide mark, tube worms are hidden beneath the sand. Only their jelly-like egg masses stick out from the tough tubes they have built. Swimming crabs and tiny pale fish try to hide beneath the clear water. Wading birds wander among the little sand-dwelling creatures. Here, where the beach meets the tropical seas, their long bills probe the sand for their meals.

A mangrove island

Along the tidal marshes of the Caribbean, fresh water from the land mixes with warm, salty sea-water. Mangrove trees grow in vast swamps and make tiny islands in these shallow, salty waters. Their unusual roots allow the mangrove trees to grow in such muddy areas.

From a distance, a mangrove island appears to be on stilts. These are in fact the arching roots of the red mangroves. They help to prop up the trees in the muddy tidal waters. Red mangroves also have long, thin aerial roots which dangle from the branches.

As you approach the mangrove island, you might see an osprey perched in the branches, ready to swoop down to catch a fish. Herons, egrets, bitterns and other wading birds may be feeding among the arching roots. A closer look reveals many small creatures living there, including shrimps, crabs and fish. Barnacles, oysters and nerite snails live on the algae-covered roots. They open up to feed when the high tide covers them, and close up tight as the tide goes out.

To explore the interior of the island, you must climb over arching roots and fallen, rotting logs. The carpet of slippery mud and decaying leaves will ooze around your feet. Under the dense cover of the treetops, only small patches of sunlight filter through. Within the swamp it is cool and damp. Sounds and smells surround you. Hawks, cuckoos and other birds call in the distance. There is a constant chirping of crickets and buzzing of mosquitoes. Butterflies flutter by and many small animals, such as squirrels, lizards and crabs, can be heard scurrying through the trees.

Deeper in the swamp, the red mangroves become mixed with black mangroves. The black mangroves have special breathing roots. These stick up through the mud, and surround the trees. In this region of the swamp, the smell of sulphur fills the air. It is produced by the special bacteria that live in this mud, which has no oxygen.

Many creatures are found on the swamp floor. Coffee bean snails, termites and roaches live among decaying leaves and rotting logs. Other animals live in the holes that dot the swamp floor. Smaller holes may be homes for fiddler crabs. Giant land crabs or swamp rats may live in the larger holes, and come out at night to search for food.

The white mangroves are found in the driest regions of the swamp, far from the tidal waters. They do not have special roots for living in wet, muddy areas. White mangroves look like ordinary trees, but can survive in salty water brought by occasional storm tides.

Right Mangrove swamps in Florida's everglades. Notice how the clumps of mangrove trees look like islands on stilts.

9 EXPLORING THE ISLANDS

Today many of the people of the Caribbean are relatively poor. Lack of natural resources and fertile land combined with a high population have in some cases led to this poverty. However, there is always a big welcome for the tourist. To visit the islands we might travel by ship, small boat, aircraft or even sea-plane if the island is too small or rocky to have an airport. There are many beautiful beaches on which we could sunbathe and the warm, clear water is ideal for scuba-diving, water-skiing, sailing or exploring the coral reefs.

The scenery varies greatly from island to island. There are flat, infertile fields where poor farmers have difficulty growing crops, and mountainous regions with steaming tropical rain forests. Colourful parrots, lizards and frogs would be just some of the tropical wildlife we might see. Exotic plants such as the hibiscus, bougainvillaea, and wild orchids fill gardens and fields. In the lowlands there are plantations of sugar cane and bananas.

As tourists we would have a vast number of exciting places to visit and things to do. We

Below Dense vegetation slopes down to the sea at Balandra Bay on the Atlantic coast of Trinidad.

could visit one of the farms on the Cayman Islands where young turtles are hatched and reared. These farms will help save the turtles from extinction and provide an additional source of meat for the islanders. On the island of Montserrat we might see an active volcano spitting out sulphurous gases. We could visit the magnificent tomb of Christopher Columbus on the island of Hispaniola, or see the flamingoes on Bonaire.

Let's take a closer look at the way of life on four of the larger islands: Cuba, Haiti, Jamaica

Below Flamingo stands protectively over its young on Bonaire Island.

Above Cigars from Havana, Cuba, are considered to be the best in the world. This experienced cigar maker is allowed to smoke while working.

and Trinidad. Yoù can see them on the map. Cuba is larger than all the other islands put together and has about one-third of the total population. Originally a Spanish farming colony, most of the land is flat enough for cultivation. There are sugar plantations and factories for processing the sugar. Another important crop is tobacco. Cigars made in Havana, the capital of Cuba, are considered the best in the world.

Haiti is very mountainous and the soil is infertile. It has a large population but few resources and is therefore one of the poorest countries in the world. The religion of the local people is Voodoo, a kind of black magic, based

Above Tumbledown shacks in the poverty-stricken area of Port-au-Prince, capital of Haiti. Haiti is one of the poorest countries in the world.

on a mixture of African superstitions and Christianity. It is said that Voodoo priests and priestesses conduct strange dances and ceremonies. Inland, the mountains of Haiti are very beautiful and it is sometimes possible to see crocodiles in the rivers.

Jamaica is a wealthier island. It exports bauxite, which is used to make aluminium, and so sugar and bananas, which are the basic exports of other Caribbean islands, are not so important here. Much of the scenery of Jamaica is very beautiful, but to gain a complete picture of the island, we should also see the shanty towns around the capital, Kingston. These were built by poor people looking for work in the city. Jamaica has an exciting history

Above A colourful scene during Trinidad's annual carnival.

for it used to be a base for the pirates and smugglers who once roamed the Caribbean.

Trinidad and Tobago are the southernmost islands of the Windward chain. They are better off than some of their neighbours because oil has recently been discovered in their coastal waters. Trinidad also sells asphalt, which is made from pitch found in a natural lake on the island and is used to surface roads. But Trinidad and Tobago are probably best known for their steel bands. February is carnival time. The bands play, people dress up in colourful costumes and everyone dances for days without stopping.

The Panama Canal

Explorers in the New World quickly realized that only a very narrow strip of land, the Isthmus of Panama, separated the Caribbean from the Pacific Ocean. By the nineteenth century a great deal of trade was carried between the Atlantic and Pacific Oceans. If a canal could be dug across the Isthmus to join the Pacific with the Caribbean Sea, how much easier it would be to sail 82 kilometres (51 miles) across Panama than around the gale-swept seas of Cape Horn. In 1880 a French company began trying to dig a canal across Panama. They were soon in difficulties because hundreds of their workers died from yellow fever and malaria. Soon the French had to give up.

Then, in 1903, the United States signed a treaty with Panama which allowed them to try digging a canal. In 1904 the work began. This time an Army doctor named Walter Gorgas

Below Steam shovel at work on the Panama Canal in the early years of this century.

Above Modern freighter steams through the Panama Canal.

took charge of the disease problems. He had learned that mosquitoes spread yellow fever and malaria. By working very hard to kill the mosquitoes and destroy their breeding grounds he was able to do away with both yellow fever and malaria along the Panama Canal. The Canal was finished in 1914.

It is 82 kilometres (51 miles) long and passes through a large lake called Lake Gatun. Because the land is higher than the sea, locks were built at each end of the Canal. These locks are like small, square lakes with big gates at each end. A ship is towed into the lock and the gates are closed. The lock is then filled with water so that the ship rises 27 metres (85 ft) to the level of the Canal. When a ship leaves the Canal at the other end it must enter a lock and be lowered 27 metres! In 1970 over 15,500 ships passed through the Canal.

The bustling ports

Most of the important industrial ports of these two seas are found on the northern shores of the Gulf of Mexico. The largest are in the states of Alabama, Texas, Mississippi and Louisiana in the southern part of the United States. The purpose of the ports is to provide the facilities for ships to load and unload goods so that trade can take place. Although the ports of the Gulf are very different they all share this basic function.

Mobile, Alabama, still bears traces of its French and Spanish origins. It did not become an important port until the opening of the Panama Canal in 1914. Mobile's main exports are timber, naval supplies, cotton and various manufactured products. Incoming freighters bring aluminium ore and agricultural products from South America.

The seaports of Texas provide deep water harbours for large, ocean-going ships. The economy of Texas is partly based on oil, and it is the largest producer of livestock in the United States. Cotton is also very important. Other natural resources exported from Texas are sulphur, helium, salt and cement. Houston is the biggest port in Texas and it deals with a huge volume of shipping every year. Corpus Christi is also a big industrial seaport, but its mild climate and beautiful beaches make it a popular tourist resort too. The public marina is home to thousands of pleasure boats in which holiday makers explore the Gulf and its islands. In April every year Corpus Christi has a big festival called Buccaneer Days.

The state of Louisiana exports many farm products such as sweet potatoes, rice, sugar, cotton and strawberries. New Orleans is the state's biggest port, but it is also a beautiful city. Its night-clubs and bars were the birth-place of jazz in the 1920s and 1930s. In the historic French Quarter you can visit Pirate's Alley, which is a narrow side street where many local artists sell their work. At the French market you can visit the open-air vegetable and seafood stalls, and see the places where slaves were once put up for sale.

Right Royal Avenue in the French Quarter, New Orleans.

Below The docks at New Orleans, on the Mississippi River.

Ships of all kinds

The lives of the people of the Caribbean and Gulf of Mexico are closely tied to the sea. Boats are used to get from one island to another; large cruise ships bring tourists from other countries; and freighters come and go with their valuable cargoes.

One of the bigger ships which ploughs to and fro across the Caribbean and the Gulf is the oil tanker. These ships are made up of a series of storage areas which carry oil or methane. Tankers are often more than 300 metres (980 ft) long, and can weigh up to 212,000 tonnes. A new type of vessel which is being used today is the 'container ship'. The cargo is placed in steel boxes and hauled on and off the ship by a tall crane. This type of ship is faster to load than older types of freighter, but expensive to build. Cargo freighters are still used to move some kinds of dry cargo – coal, bananas or coffee for example.

The cruise ships which carry thousands of tourists on holidays around the Caribbean are

Below Wooden fishing vessels off the coast of Haiti.

Above Large cruise ships bring tourists to Nassau Island in the Bahamas.

Below Wooden canoes are used for fishing close inshore in many parts of the Caribbean.

big and luxurious, and provide many activities for their guests. They generally carry between 400 and 700 passengers.

The wooden boats of the islanders are a means of livelihood as well as transport. The sailing craft are made by hand to traditional designs which may vary from one island to the next. Most boats are designed to serve as work boats, but some are also made for racing. They are planked with wood from island forests, and built with simple hand tools. Delighted tourists like to watch these hard-working boats unload their silvery catches of fish, shrimp or conch at the quay sides. These lovely little boats have won the admiration of sailors around the world.

Glossary

Algae   A type of large seaweed.

Asphalt   A tarry mixture used to make a smooth, hard surface on roads and paths.

Barnacle   A small shellfish which clings to rocks and the bottom of ships.

Bauxite   A clay-like aluminium ore (originally found at Les Baux in southern France). Used to make aluminium.

Container ships   Fast cargo boats which carry their goods packed in large containers rather than loose.

Continental drift   The movement of landmasses of the world towards or away from each other.

Coral   Stony, skeletal structure formed in masses by simple marine animals (polyps). It is found in various colours and sometimes builds up into coral reefs.

Current   The flow of water in a given direction. In the Cairibbn the strongest currents are the North and South Equatorial Currents.

Fossil   The remains, impression or trace of a plant or animal found preserved in rock.

Helium   A very light gas – used in balloons and airships.

Hurricane   A violent tropical wind storm travelling at over 120 km/h.

Lagoon   A shallow, salt-water lake connected to the sea.

Larva   A grub or an insect after it has left the egg but before it turns into an adult.

Lava   Molten rock which flows down the sides of a volcano, then cools and solidifies.

Limestone   A kind of rock or sand composed chiefly of calcium carbonate.

Lock   An enclosure in a canal for raising or lowering boats from one level to another.

Mid-Atlantic Ridge   Range of underwater mountains in the centre of the Atlantic.

Mangrove   A tree which grows in vast swamps in salty, shallow waters along the tidal marshes of the Caribbean. There are several varieties.

OTEC   Ocean Thermal Electric Conversion device. A power-plant built to generate electricity by exploiting the variation in temperature between the different layers of the ocean.

Parasite   An animal or plant which lives on another and takes food from it without giving any benefit in return.

Pitch   Thick, black, tar-like substance which can occur naturally in 'pitch lakes' or is obtained by boiling down coal tar.

Plankton   Tiny animals (zooplankton) and plants (phytoplankton) which drift in millions through the seas.

Plates   Bands of rock about 65 kilometres deep which move very slowly over the core of the Earth carrying the seas and the continents with them.

Polyp   A simple coral animal which can divide and multiply.

Quartz   A common rock found in transparent crystals. Some quartz (such as the purple amethyst) is coloured.

Salinity   Saltiness. The salinity of sea-water varies a little according to the depth of the water and its distance from the Poles.

Sediments   Clay, sand and silt which collect on the sea floor and may become hard rocks. Remains of dead animals are also incorporated into the sediments.

Sulphur   A yellow, non-metallic element, used in making (for example) matches, gunpowder, sulphuric acid.

Termite   A pale, ant-like insect which eats wood.

Tidal wave   A great wave (often caused by an earthquake under the sea) which can destroy coastal towns and villages. They are also called tsunami waves.

Tide   The rise and fall of the sea which usually occurs twice a day.

Trench   An area on the sea floor where two plates meet and one moves under or over another.

Above An ocean paradise. Fishing boats sail into a golden sunset off the coast of Haiti.

The people who wrote this book

Pat Hargreaves Marine biologist, Institute of Oceanographic Sciences, Surrey (General Editor).

Professor Lowell P. Thomas Marine scientist. Professor of Biological Oceanography, Rosenstiel School of Marine and Atmospheric Science, University of Miami.

Genevieve S. Craig Graduate student, Marine Geology and Geophysics Division, Rosenstiel School of Marine and Atmospheric Science, University of Miami.

Stephanie G. Baker Administrator, Marine Laboratory, Rosenstiel School of Marine and Atmospheric Science, University of Miami.

H. S. Noel Journalist in fisheries and marine subjects.

Kim E. Harrison Research assistant. Noyes Fellow, Rosenstiel School of Marine and Atmospheric Science, Miami.

S. C. Pitcher Teacher of Geography, King's College School, London.

Index

Books to read

Angel, M. and H., *Ocean Life* (Octopus Books)

Cochrane, J., *The Amazing World of the Sea* (Angus & Robertson)

Jones, A. *Marine life of the Caribbean* (Macmillan)

Keeling, C. H., *Under the Sea* (F. Watts)

Lambert, D., *The Oceans* (Ward Lock)

Merret, N., *The How and Why Wonder Book of the Deep Sea* (Transworld)

Parsons, J., *Oceans* (Macdonald Educational)

Saunders, G. D., *Spotters' Guide to Seashells* (Usborne)

Stonehouse, B., *The Living World of the Sea* (Hamlyn)

Picture acknowledgements

Heather Angel 42, 47, 49; Ardea Photos 48; Allan Cash 9, 33, 57, 65; Bruce Coleman, by the following photographers: Jen & Des Bartlett 45; S. C. Bisserot 46; Jane Burton 44, 54, 51; Alain Compost 37; M. P. L. Fogden 8; Gordon Langsbury 55; M. P. Kahl 39; NASA 25; Timothy O'Keefe 16, 38, 40, 43; Robert Schroeder 51; Bill Wood 33; Van Wormer 59; G. Ziesler 52–3; Colour Library International 14, 23, 41; Bill Donohoe 10–11; J. Gibb 58, 61; Alan Hutchison 26, 63, 66, 69; Intersub 13; Anna Jupp 15; Mansell Collection 18, 20, 21, 62; John Mitchell 12, 27; Seaphot 19 (below), 30, 34; Shell 36; John Topham 9, 24, 31, 60, 64, 67 (both); Wayland Picture Library 19 (above), 22; Zefa *front cover, title page*, 7, 29.